AUTOMOBILIA

13   Automobiles

Text ©   Peter Card
Illustration ©   Phillips Fine Art
            Auctioneers
Edited by   Emma Sinclair-Webb
Designed by   Strange Design Associates

Copyright © Dunestyle Publishing Ltd and
Boxtree Ltd, 1989

Boxtree Ltd.
36 Tavistock Street
London WC2 7PB

Conceived by Dunestyle Publishing Ltd

ISBN 1 85283 250 9

Typesetting by O'Reilly Clark, London
Colour separation by Chroma Graphics
(Overseas) Pte Ltd
Printed In Italy by New Interlitho spa.

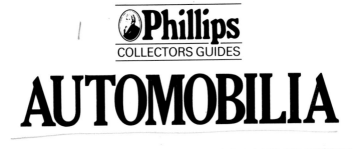

Phillips
COLLECTORS GUIDES

AUTOMOBILIA

PETER CARD

BOXTREE

Phillips, founded in 1796, has a
reputation for specialisation. Its
specialists handle fine art, antiques
and collectors' items under more than
60 subject headings — a huge
spectrum of art and artefacts that
ranges from Old Masters and the finest
antique furniture to cigarette cards
and comparatively modern pop
memorabilia. The auction group's
Collectors' Centre, situated at Phillips
West Two in Salem Road, Bayswater,
London, is constantly recognising,
defining and catering for new trends
in collecting. It answers hundreds of
queries a day from collectors,
museums, dealers and the public at
large. The shelves of its cataloguing
halls are packed with a treasure-trove
of objects, awaiting their turn to appear
at auction. To varying extents, the
scene there and in the main Mayfair
salerooms (Phillips, 7 Blenheim Street,
London W1Y 0AS; telephone 01-629
6602) is repeated at a score of Phillips
branches elsewhere in Britain.

Phillips West 2
10 Salem Road
London W2 4BU
Telephone: 01-221 5303

Contents

Introduction

Having once been the most casual of collecting spheres, automobilia is now one of the fastest growing hobbies, with what would appear to be a never ending supply of assorted memorabilia to catch the avid collector's eye.

The collector today is motivated by rather different aspirations than the well-travelled, old-style collector of the past. The one stimulus that dominates above all others is, of course, nostalgia – that sentimentality experienced by collectors of all ages. 'Nostalgia is big business', so most experts will tell us; but why?

Certainly, as far as motoring is concerned, we all have memories of those halcyon days of our youth, made up of enjoyable experiences such as trips to the seaside or out with the family on picnic sorties. It may also be memories of watching with thrilled enjoyment the first motor race or hill climb, and the exhilaration of trying out those driving techniques in one's newly acquired second-hand car. My own memories are deeply set with motorcycle trips on scorching, sunny days to Hayling Island or being driven in a Standard Nine convertible through tree-lined roads so tightly packed that the creation was practically a tunnel; and so to the present when my third daughter was born in the passenger seat of the family car, while recklessly travelling at 82 m.p.h. in the direction of the maternity hospital; such memories are dreams made of.

What then is automobilia? Basically it is any item that is associated with the motor vehicle, whether it be motorcycle, car or lorry, from its very earliest days to the present. It can take the form of sales brochures, photographs and magazines to hardware such as mascots, badges, radiators and lighting equipment; indeed practically anything short of a complete vehicle itself.

In a book of this size it will not be possible to cover all the aspects of the wide automobilia field. However, I will try to cover the more popular collecting areas and perhaps supply enough information to whet the appetite of the most reluctant collector!

Below A splendid example of early Morris in
immaculate condition at a car rally.

Chapter One

Printed Literature

This category is so varied, so vast and so positively endless in its collecting possibilities that in one chapter we can barely scratch the surface. I will attempt, however, to include such headings as catalogues, magazines, competition programmes and, of course, hard-bound books, as well as covering such odd ball items as sheet music, cigarette cards and photographs.

Perhaps the most enjoyable facet of collecting such ephemera

Below A period photograph of the start of a race at Brooklands, dated 1932, with a dedication. A little research will reveal the race in question and perhaps who is driving which car. Value: £20/$36.

is the sheer choice of subject matter; better still, no matter what subject is chosen, the cost of building and continually adding to a collection can vary from practically nothing to many thousands of pounds. As a teenager, a friend started collecting the programmes and signatures of Formula One racing car drivers, and today has a fine collection that consists of art, comment and memories from some of the world's most famous people. All it has cost him is patience, persuasion and downright audacity, and he is still adding to his collection today. On the other hand, another collector of my acquaintance only collects first edition motoring books published before 1914 and has spent a considerable sum of money doing so. His collection is superb and a delight to inspect. Which man has the better collection is not in the least important, what is significant is that each enjoys collecting and their own collections and finds pleasure in sharing the interest with others.

Where would the motor car be today without the supporting literature that, by necessity, has flooded onto the market? From the earliest days, when Daimler advertised his tricycle in 1888, to a hundred years later, when the Motor Show at the N.E.C. spawns a whole new breed of car, supporting sales brochures have been all important.

Bound Books

Articles about motor cars have been printed in magazines, such as the *English Mechanic*, since the days when Gurney's steam carriage ventured onto the streets in 1827. However, it is thought that the first bound book on the subject is Knight's *Notes on Motor Carriages*, with Lockert's *Les Voitures à Pétrole* being printed in France at about the same time in 1896. Both books today will, even in poor condition, cost a king's ransom. Technical books were not popular with Victorian and Edwardian automobilists, who much preferred the travel-logs and general interest books which seemed to abound before the Great War. *Through Persia in a Motor Car* by Claude Anet is one

Below A wealth of motoring periodicals have been printed over the years, presenting today's enthusiast with a wide choice. Established collectors have their particular favourites, usually magazines like *The Motor* or *Autocar*; this author has a penchant for *The Motor Trader* because of the detailed articles that present a who's who to the trade, as well as bankruptcy proceedings and patent information. Value: from a few pence to £20/a few cents to $36 each.

such book. Bound in buckram and embossed in gold, with a coloured motoring scene on the front cover, the book was published in 1907 and describes a journey comprising ten people in a 40 HP Mercedes, 20 HP Mercedes and a 16 HP Fiat from Bucharest to Constantinople. As is usual in this period, the content smacks of upper class complacency and, unfortunately, the vehicles do not feature very much in the text. A good copy should be bought for about £10/$18.

One aspect of book collecting that I enjoy is finding and researching 'association copies'. These are books that have been personalized by their owner or author, perhaps by the addition of written corrections in the margin or, as in the case of *Motor Days in England* by the American, John Dillon (1908), a rather odd inscription by the author. Addressed to a Mr Fraser, he wrote, 'sincere regards and esteem even after death'. Having read the fourth chapter, it became clear that Mr. Fraser was a man known to the author and, at the time, reading between the lines, had an incurable disease. A little research establishes the gentleman's address and the fact that he died before he received the book; this dedication adds, in my view, an extra dimension to an otherwise benign and pedestrian book. Copies should be found for about £5/$9.

But, far and away the cream of travelling books must be Luigi Barzini's *Pekin to Paris* (note the spelling change), being an account of Prince Borghese's journey across two continents in an Italia motor car. The journey was, in fact, an epic race of five cars under the auspices of *Le Matin*, the French newspaper. Revived and republished in

Overleaf If they have been kept out of the sun, the definition and contrast of Victorian and Edwardian photographs is excellent. The photograph shows a 4 hp or 6 hp tiller steered Daimler in Great Yarmouth in about 1898. Value: £20/$36, depending on size.

recent years, copies of the original 1907 work, with coloured, embossed cover and tipped-in map, will command £20/$36 or more at auction.

Scrutiny of the second-hand book stalls, not least the odd jumble sale or two, will often produce some motoring classics for a few pence. I treasure my *Boys Book of the Motor Car* by John Harrison (Oxford University Press 1926), with dust cover which I picked up in a local car boot sale recently for 25p. A similar book also appealing to the young enthusiast is the *Motor Cycle Book for Boys* (Ilife and Sons 1928) prepared by the staff of *The Motor Cycle* magazine. My copy was given to me many years ago and was possibly the guiding light to my interest today, but how many more worthy souls has the same book influenced over the years? It discusses in simple language a wide range of topics, covering the principles of brake horse power, petrol consumption, road manners and the joy of motoring. The coloured illustrations of the 'characteristics and colour schemes of the modern cycle tanks' are a joy to behold and well worth the £30-£40/$54-$72 you will need to pay for a good example.

Sales Catalogues and Brochures

Perhaps the most universally popular and the most prevalent of all motoring literature, catalogues fall into two subtle but, nevertheless, different categories.

Sales catalogues are issued by the manufacturer or retailer and describe his products in detail, together with the appropriate illustrations and text; they can range, for example, from a 1910 Brown Brothers' catalogue, jam-packed with illustrations of motoring accessories (value about £50/$90), to a two page (1959)

catalogue describing the salient technical details and body styles of the Bond mini car.

The other category is termed sales brochures. These are very much more glossy affairs with plenty of illustrations, usually in colour, but only advertising one particular variety of car. Various body styles can be shown and various sizes of engine listed, but it is basically a one car advertisement. For example, an opening broadsheet of this type, advertising the M.G. T series of 1949, would command a value of £25/$45, whereas a brochure depicting the Jaguar SS 80 and SS 100 models would set you back £200/$360 or more, depending on its condition.

Photographs

An excellent source of enjoyment, early photographs can give a glimpse of motoring pleasures of days past, and some amusement can be had trying to pin-point the place of exposure, as well as identifying the various vehicles. Still to be found in considerable numbers today, with interesting, unpublished images in seemingly endless supply,

J & C.COOPER.

COACH BUILDERS'& WH

photographs fall into two main categories for the collector:

(a) The printed postcard photograph was very popular, particularly prior to 1914. Individual photographs would be printed to order at the request of a local club, perhaps in celebration of their charabanc outing to the coast. On the other hand, a set of postcards of a young man astride his motorcycle could be supplied for his personal use. The variations of this medium seem to be endless and a good selection can

Below Dating from about 1904, the quality and detail of the early artwork in this *Coach Builders' and Wheelwrights' Art Journal* (18 pages) is excellent. Value: £40/$72.

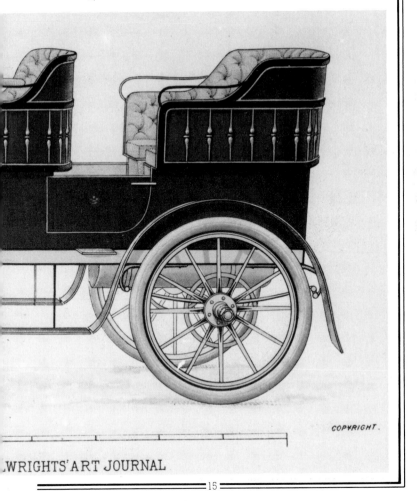

COPYRIGHT.

LWRIGHTS' ART JOURNAL

always be bought from postcard auctions, varying in value from 50p to £20/90 cents to $36 each. Given people's morbid fascination for disasters, postcard photographs depicting vehicle accidents seem to be the most popular.

(b) The standard black and white photographs, of course, survive in vast numbers. While it must be said all photographs depicting vehicles are of interest to the collector, albeit their conditon may be poor, some illustrations are very much more interesting, and therefore more valuable, than others. For example Uncle Sid standing next to his newly acquired Morris Eight may be a worthy photograph, (particularly if some information about the time and place of exposure is recorded on the back) and is worth keeping, but will only have a minimal value. On the other hand, a photograph of some of the competitors in the 1896 Emancipation Run to Brighton, or of Malcolm Campbell's home workshops, taken in 1932 at Little Gattan near Reigate, are of great historical importance, both as source material for the historian and instant nostalgia for the collector. It is not unusual for an album of photographs of this latter type to achieve in excess of £300/$540 at auction.

What is of paramount importance when dealing with early photographs is that they be treated with care. Not only should they be kept out of sunlight, but a very damaged and sorry example can be protected by backing with card and carefully covering with cling-film. There are also specialists who will produce copies, which can be particularly useful if you wish to have enlargements made, so that the less obvious details become clearer.

ARS

MADE
IN THE
·WORLD'S
GREATEST
ENGINEERING
CENTRE

G C⁰Y L™
DGETON·GLASGOW.

Left A rare Argyll Motor Cars instruction manual for 8 hp to 20 hp cars and commercial vehicles, with colour illustrations and period text. Value: £100-£120/$180-$220.

Magazines

The first British weekly motoring magazine, appearing in November 1895, was *The Autocar*. Although not the first magazine of this type it was certainly the most successful, particularly before the First War. Good clean early copies today are quite rare, with the special edition printed in red upon the repeal of the Locomotives on Highways Act being, perhaps, the rarest. More often than not magazines would be sent to the publishers for binding every half year and, unfortunately, the covers and advertisement pages would often be discarded. Today, however, the value of a bound volume is more than doubled if these items have been left intact, a half year volume being worth between £50 and £150/$90-$270, depending upon the condition.

Motoring Illustrated and *The Car Illustrated* were both quality magazines launched upon the tide of enthusiasm for the new breed of motorist, in *circa* 1910, which have unfortunately disappeared.

Motor Sport commenced publication in 1924 and, as the name implies, was directed at the race-going public. Early volumes, however, are very rare and volumes 2, 3 and 4 were recently sold at auction for £2,600/$4,680. Bound volumes are still in plentiful supply today, from bookstalls, and an unbroken run from, say, 1935 to 1955, could be collected for a few hundred pounds.

Magazines from more recent years are also eminently collectable, with *Veteran and Vintage* magazine (founded in 1956) and *Old Motor* (although now defunct) still in plentiful supply and an excellent source of reading.

With motoring magazines there is one issue that is more enthusiastically sought than any other printed each year: this is the 'show number'. Printed in October, in celebration of the year's Motor Show, it contains advertisements and articles covering all that was best in the current motor industry; consequently these particular issues represent an excellent history of the development of the motor car.

Competition Programmes

Like the badges, Brooklands 'Official Race Cards' are keenly

sought by collectors. In fact these were not cards at all, but small 8vo size paper-backed books detailing, amongst the advertisements, drivers and entrants for that day's racing, previous winners, facilities at the clubhouse, new 'bright stars', etc. Cards from the 1920s are hard to find these days and, depending on condition, will fetch between £15 and £30/$27-$54 each. The more colourful wraps of the later editions are more prevalent, but will often fetch £20/$36 or more at auction.

Competition programmes were also supplied for hill climbs and lesser speed and road racing events (the law forbids road racing in England). These, too, are most interesting, particularly if you live near sites like Donington, Shelsey Walsh, Brighton or Saltburn Sands; a good collection of local interest literature can still be put together for quite a modest sum.

Sources of Supply

I never cease to be amazed at where literature of all types can be found. If one is persistent, the standard hunting grounds like jumble sales, boot sales and the odd junk shop, which, alas, has all but disappeared from the back street scene, can produce some interesting gems. I was amused to hear recently of a cache of *Industrial Motor* being offered for sale by the local pawn shop and several issues of Coopers' *Coachbuilders* being offered by the district undertakers.

Left A damaged glass plate negative was recently given to me and after taking it to my local photographers I found the positive photograph was of a most unusual vehicle of unknown make. Help was at hand, however, through the excellent services of the Veteran Car Club of Great Britain Newsletter. The photograph was published and more knowledgeable members were able to identify the vehicle as a 1906 Armstrong-Whitworth armoured car, designed by W. G. Wilson. The many existing car clubs are able to provide such specialist help. Value of the negative: £10/$18.

Below RAF fire-tender manufactured by Albion. Note the brass temperature gauge and bolt-down water cap on the radiator grille.

Chapter Two

Advertising

The promotion of one's products or services is as old as the demands of good business acumen. The Victorians achieved a mastery of advertising that started with the Great Exhibition of 1851 and has continued and diversified into the many and varied forms that, today, we tend to take entirely for granted.

Before the days of an established motoring press, companies like Benz, Daimler and De Dion would have printed on cheap pulp paper broadsheets depicting an illustration of their products, together with some facts and figures, to include the range of models available, engine sizes, body styles, and sometimes the price! These sheets would often be sent through the post, unsolicited, to likely customers (in the same way that today's junk mail invades our homes). Needless to say, these broadsheets are extremely rare today and, in the unlikely event that an example should turn up at auction, you will need to visit your bank manager.

The student of early advertising can confirm that it was not at all unusual for entrepreneurs and manufacturers to espouse wild claims and outrageous statements, in an effort to promote their products to a naïve and gullible public. The motor trade was certainly no exception; take, for example, Edward Joel Pennington, who claimed that his motor tricycle had the ability to fly fully laden across a ravine!

Magazine Advertisements

Although the infant motoring press undoubtedly received vast amounts of revenue from advertisements, other more social magazines also had advertisements placed in them. Good examples can be found in the *Ironmonger*, *Hearth and Home*, *Illustrated London News* and *The Sphere* and will provide a good source of reference for those collectors interested in the styles and blandishments of this period. Unfortunately, you will find most magazines of this age showing their years, with covers and editorial perhaps torn or missing. These often turn up in jumbled bundles, having just been cleared out from lofts or outhouses, and I have seen several excellent scrap books made up of such material, which otherwise would have been useless to a magazine collector.

It is also true to say that throughout this century publicity and advertising have been very spirited. Until the early 1920s illustrations of the products for sale, rather than text, tended to dominate. However Edward S. Jordan, the manufacturer of the Jordan motor car, will be best remembered today as the man who broke away from this 'nuts and bolts' advertising. He introduced a spirit of emotional appeal into the advertising of his vehicles and over the years his advertisements have become

Below Two modern reproductions of earlier enamel signs advertising New Hudson motorcycles and Duesenberg luxury cars. Notice the absence of rust marks or chipping, which would be most unusual in an original sign.

more famous than his cars, which ceased production during the Depression in 1931. The peak of his advertising genius must surely be his 'Somewhere West of Laramie', which first appeared in the *Saturday Evening Post* of 1923: 'Somewhere west of Laramie there's a bronco-busting, steer-roping girl who knows what I'm talking about. She can tell what a sassy pony, that's a cross between greased lightning and the place where it hits, can do with eleven hundred pounds of steel and action when he's going high, wide and handsome. The truth is – The Playboy was built for her . . .'

Throughout the 1920s and 30s advertising in periodicals became more subtle and colourful. Professional artists were employed to use their skills in the most provocative and spirited way and, today, a framed and glazed collection of illustrations from the

pen of such names as Roy Nockolds, John Hassal, Peter Helck, Jean Routier and many others will make a most wonderful display. Obtainable in the same way as described earlier, it must not be forgotten that other publications such as *Country Life*, *The Field*, and *Horse and Hound* also carry superbly reproduced vehicle advertisements.

By its very nature, of course, original art work for advertising is

Left One of a set of four advertising cards for Castrol Oil, published and issued to garages between 1927 and 1937. This example depicts Henry Segrave in the land speed record-breaking Sunbeam of 1927. The 51 cm x 35½ cm (20 in x 14 in) card is superbly coloured and of high artistic merit. Value: £100-£150/$180-$270 each.

Below A well-shaped Karpal car polish enamel sign, designed in the Art Deco style with the firm's colours. Some chipping and damage to the enamel can be seen on the base and sides. Value: £80/$144.

seldom seen in the market place today. The low survival rate for this type of material probably rests with the magazine publishers who seldom returned source material to its artist and, more often than not, threw it out with the rubbish after a brief period in storage.

Enamel Signs

No other advertising ploy has had more impact upon the buying public than the enamel sign. This is not just because they were often colourful, or because they were placed in very visible places, or that many were exceedingly well designed and shaped. The reason is more subtle, in many cases so subtle that the promoting companies themselves never fully appreciated their worth. To affix to a wall a very hard-finished and weather-resistant advertisement gave it an air of permanence and stability that, by its nature, implied that the company or product being advertised also was 'here to stay' and safe to use.

Alas, the days of the enamel sign have almost gone, but it is extraordinary how many have survived and, if the number that turn up regularly in automobilia sales is anything to go by, they are still being found. Generally square or oblong in shape, signs advertising petrol and oil are least rare, with auction prices varying between £10 and £100/$18-$180, depending on condition. A 'Pratts' Perfection Spirit' would be

finished in black, yellow and red enamels and has become synonymous with that company. Castrol, on the other hand, used green, black and red, with BP preferring a most attractive blue again supported by red and black.

Signs advertising motor car manufacturers are perhaps the most sought-after. Morris, Jaguar and Humber issued a wide variety, but rarities such as Hotchkiss, Clyno and Trojan signs will set the pulse of any avid

Left Prestigious car showrooms often required something just a little bit better than the standard cardboard cut-out or show card. This well-crafted leaping Jaguar bronze stands 61 cm (2 ft) high and would have been supplied by Jaguar to embellish a Jaguar distributor's showroom during the 1950s. Due to the cost of manufacture, few models of this type would have been issued, so its appearance at auction is a rare site. Value: £500-£600/$900-$1,080.

collector racing.

Although their heat-hardened gloss finish weathered very well indeed, many signs have, unfortunately, borne the brunt of small boys with stones or air rifles, not to mention a clumsy fitter knocking small flakes of enamel off during erection. This, then, exposes the tin backing and allows oxydization to take its toll; so, if today you are offered a clean unchipped example, do check that it is not a reproduction! A sign that has acquired a few knocks and dents over the years, in my view, is enhanced by the wrinkles of age and as long as the central illustration and wording are intact it should be a valuable addition to any collection.

Branded Trade Gifts

In support of their standard advertising, vehicle manufacturing companies produced, throughout the 20s and 30s, many cheap but useful gifts for promotional purposes. These were often given to retailers or dealerships, and sometimes good clients, and usually took the form of cigarette boxes, ashtrays, penknives and letter openers, always with the name of the supplying company attached to the gift somewhere.

The Motor Show and Christmas season were the occasions for presenting these gifts. Many were simply company mascots mounted on a block of marble and called a paperweight while others were

Above left A good and rare MG enamel sign
showing signs of damage to the edge, but with the
main content left intact. Value: £50-£100/$90-$180.

Above The French sculptor F. Bazin inscribed all the
examples of the stork mascot he designed for use
on Hispano-Suiza motor cars after the Great War. It
is, however, rare for a desk piece, which was
supplied as an advertising trade gift, to be similarly
signed. Value: £300-£500/$540-$900.

mounted on blocks of wood and called book-ends.

The most prestigious series of trade gifts ever supplied during this period were those given by Rolls Royce between the years 1926 and 1932. Each year they gave away to their most worthy distributors a single solid silver desk piece incorporating the 'spirit of ecstasy' mascot. In 1926 it was an ashtray, in 1927 an inkwell, 1928 a clock, 1929 a cigarette box, and so on. Had the distributor worked hard during this period, he would have been the proud

MOTOCYCLES COTTE

Affiches BELLEVILLE, Grande Imprimerie de Montrouge, PARIS

owner of the full set comprised of paper knife, ink blotter and pen tray. Such is the enthusiasm for Rolls Royce memorabilia of this type that, today, a full set of seven pieces will sell for over £5,000/ $9,000 at auction.

Left This mildly amusing lithographic poster advertising Cottereau motorcycles is clearly signed 'René Vincent' and dated 1905. Early posters of this type are often well-detailed. Indeed, one can clearly see the chain-wheel, carburettor, ignition control, total loss oil system, oil feed and a most unusual sprung front fork arrangement, 160 cm x 116 cm (63 in x 45½ in), linen backed. Value: £300-£500/ $540-$900.

Chapter Three

Posters, Prints and Pictures

Posters

Since the industrial revolution, posters have been used as an effective method of advertising and communication. Institutions and commerce have used this medium to such effect that a great many posters have, in their time, become 'standards' which modern advertising agencies now aspire to. Who has not winced at Kitchener's finger telling you 'Your country needs you' or John Hassel's 'Jolly Fisherman' telling us 'It's so bracing at Skegness'?

The motoring industry has a long tradition of generating the most striking yet subtle images encouraging you to use this or that petrol, drive a Mercedes 'to give you class' or buy a Railton and have 'chariots lighter than air'.

The overriding joy of collecting posters is the sheer wealth of available material on offer. Like so many collecting areas it would be wise to specialize in some theme; a make of car, a petrol company, a particular artist perhaps: all will make a worthy collection. Generally speaking, posters tend to be available via dealers or auction houses; the reason for this is that many of those available today were supplied by institutions who, by design or accident, retained a stock which was duly passed on in bulk. The dealer, then, as a matter of course, will back the poster with linen to prevent (further) damage, or very often frame and glaze a particularly interesting example. Prices for these original works of art will very considerably from a few hundred pounds to several thousands. They vary in colour and artistic quality and this, together with conditon, will determine their value.

Surprisingly, size will also play its part, since the collector will want to hang his purchase in his home. Modern walls are small and very large posters are difficult to display. On the other hand; it must be said that the larger works of art, those measuring 1.7m x 1m (5ft x 3ft), are the most spectacular and exquisitely detailed.

In the early years of the century the French artists produced their best work. Names like Gamy, Montaut, Géri and René Vincent now all figure prominently in auction catalogues. The work of these artists has been extremely popular in the last 40 years and various high quality re-issues, using the original method of lithography, have been produced in limited numbers. Bearing in mind the value of the original (a period Géri will cost about £1,000/$1,800 today), these reprints are in no way inferior and can be acquired for as little as £100-£200/$180-$360.

Below Although this poster dates from 1910 the 'Michelin Man' was born in 1898 at Lyons, where the Michelin Company had a stand. Edouard Michelin's imagination was fired by a stack of tyres outside the exhibition hall and remarked, 'if it had arms it would look like a man'. This remark led to the birth of 'Mr Bibendum', a brilliant inspiration!

Prints

Before the budding collector starts looking for posters, one very important hurdle must be overcome. This is the vexed question of reproduction prints. Although sometimes very subtle, there is, nevertheless, a world of difference between an original work of art that has been lithographically reproduced as a poster, contemporary with the goods and event that it advertises, and a modern reissue of the same poster. Unfortunately, it is often not easy to distinguish between the two; colour freshness, type of paper and mode of printing all help towards identification. Needless to say, that world of difference is reflected in their value (for instance, while an original of 'Gerold's' 1932 Bugatti poster will achieve about £1,000/$1,800 at auction, one of the modern reprints will sell, framed

and glazed, for about £50/$90.) If you are in doubt, refuse to buy. Although most dealers and auction houses can be trusted to give the right advice, *caveat emptor* is more important perhaps in this category than any other.

There are now some reproduction prints which are themselves eagerly sought. The series of fifteen Monaco Grand Prix posters issued between 1930 and 1957, by artists Falcucci and Georges Ham, are regularly selling for large sums, with £6,580/$11,844 being paid recently for a 1935 example. On the other hand, a set of excellent quality post-war re-issues, which were produced in a limited edition by the original method of lithography, sell at about £1,000/$1,800 for an unmounted set.

Pictures

Original works of art fall into three main mediums: oil, watercolour and pencil/charcoal. Perhaps the earliest motoring portrait, for instance, is Henri de Toulouse-Lautrec's *'L'Automobiliste'* lithograph, measuring 10¾in x 15½in (27½ cm x 39 cm) and believed to have been executed in 1896. It is thought to be a caricature of the artist's cousin, who is shown driving a primitive car, dressed in typical attire of the period with nautical style cap, goggles, leather face mask and fur coat. Bearing in mind the previous section, this work has been copied, albeit as a rare limited edition, and these achieve about £80/$144 at auction.

Left Flights of fancy, maybe, but this rare and evocative poster advertising the 1923 series of Sitges-Barcelona races is very collectable. 51 cm x 64 cm (20 in x 25 in). Value: £150-£200/$270-$360.

Michael Wright
1922 T.T. (ISLE OF MAN)

Below A well-crafted oil on canvas, by Michael Wright, of the 3 litre Sunbeam during the 1922 Tourist Trophy, Isle of Man. Value: £1,500-£2,000/ $2,700-$3,600.

The oils of such artists as Frederick Gordon Crosby and Roy Nockolds are as popular as ever, with scenes portraying a car at speed on some foreign mountain pass or racing track being the most popular. Prices vary between £500 and £5,000/ $900-$9,000 because, like so many works of art, value is dependent on quality of craftsmanship and attention to detail; even an artist like Connally had his off-days!

Watercolour and gouache are

other popular mediums, particularly with modern artists, and the works of Dexter Brown are a *tour de force* among devotees. Other post-war artists include J. de Graffeny, Phil May, Dion Pears, Carlo Demand and Michael

Below Depicting the Isle of Man TT and the Hon. C. S. Rolls driving his Rolls Royce to victory in 1905, this oil on canvas by McConnell is dated 1964. 102 cm x 76 cm (40 in x 30 in). Value: £500-£800/ $900-$1,440.

Left A stencil overlay print with white highlighting, by Gamy, showing a racing Peugeot during the 1912 French Grand Prix. Value: £100-£200/$180-$360.

Below Vehicle artistry can be found in many forms. This is a rounding board from a small fairground ride, dating from the 1920s. The standard of execution is excellent, although the vehicle is painted with a certain amount of artistic licence! Value: £100-£200/ $180-$360.

Turner, and good examples of their work will surface from time to time.

Pencil and Charcoal

Not the most popular medium for vehicle illustration in the past, in more modern times artists have favoured pencil and charcoal for motor racing scenes, hill climbs and the like. Two artists who have espoused this medium to good effect and who died only recently are Dion Pears and Carlo Demand. As can be imagined, the medium lends itself to illustrating fast-moving cars on a rain-swept track or a dusk scene, perhaps at Le Mans or during the Mille Miglia. Prices for original work of this type are still low, so keep an eye open at the local sale rooms or gallery.

Above A coloured lithograph by Molynk, published c.1905, depicting a less than accurately drawn car breaking the speed limit; an amusing scene, nevertheless. 35 cm x 80 cm (13¾ in x 31½ in). Value: £100-£150/$180-$270.

Left A racing Bugatti on the Brooklands banking, by Roy Nockolds. Painted c.1933, this painting was once the property of Sir Malcolm Campbell and consequently its value is increased. Value: £2,000-£3,000/$3,600-$5,400.

Top left High style in 1932. The Delahaye car is coming straight at the viewer in this poster by Roger Pérot, who grabs extra effect by parallel positioning of type to horizon line.

Below left Adolphe Mouron Cassandre's 1936 poster announces that the new Simca 5 costs only 9,900 francs: a bargain! Cassandre produced stunning work on vehicles and ships.

Below A modern reproduction of an original lithographic poster by 'Gerold'. The artist has ingeniously extended the shaded presentation of the vehicle to the lettering itself. Value: £50-£150/ $90–$270.

Chapter Four

Lamps and Lighting Equipment

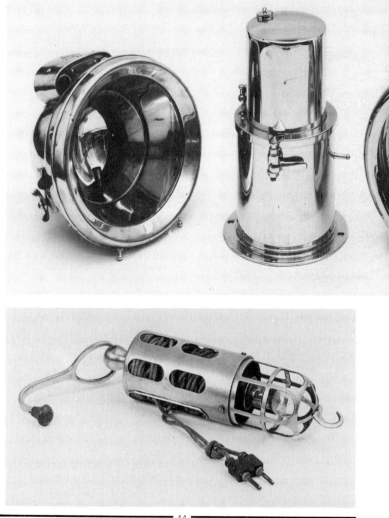

Below From left to right: (a) One of a pair of Lucas No. 673 acetylene gas projectors dating from c.1910. It will be noticed from the photograph that the Lucas designer had the foresight to include two stabilizing feet just below the front rim, to prevent tipping when not mounted on a vehicle. Also, note the porcelain burner is missing. Value £400-£600/ $720-$1,080 the pair.
(b) A large acetylene gas generator which would have been attached to the running board of a vehicle, with a rubber hose running to the front

projectors. Water is contained in the upper cylinder and this will drip onto the carbide in the lower cylinder, to create acetylene gas. Value: £100-£120/ $180-$220.
(c) One of a pair of American-manufactured Solar projectors, type 796. The centrally-mounted condenser lens can clearly be seen; this was fitted in an attempt to maximize candle power. The handle above the head ventilator is called a carrying bail. This pair recently sold for £1,100/$1,980.

Left Part of most tool kits throughout the 1920s and 1930s, this Lucas No. 96 inspection lamp is well constructed from brass; its cable would unwind to allow the plug to be pushed into the adaptor on the dashboard or firewall. Value: £20-£30/$36-$54.

Perhaps the accessories which create more interest among collectors than any other form of automobilia are the many and varied forms of lighting equipment.

Various fuel mediums were used, particularly prior tó 1920, and these include candle, oil, acetylene gas and surprisingly electricity; indeed electric lamps were available from several manufacturers from about the turn of the century. Although expensive then, their development was such that, by the early 20s, this medium was in use on 75 per cent of the motor vehicles then on the road. It was also at about this time that electric lamp design became predictable and regulated, and it therefore follows that the main period of interest to the lamp collector, as opposed to the vehicle enthusiast today, ends in that period of high inflation and manufacturing unrest after the Great War.

It is, then, the fabulous and ornate products of this earlier period that most often turn up in the auction room and on dealers' stalls. But, what were the influences involved to create this interesting variety?

Motorists, to include motor cyclists before 1900, seldom ventured out at night because their vehicles were so unreliable.

Until about 1900 candle-powered carriage lamps were often fitted to cars, purely to get them home after dark, should they be delayed by breakdowns.

Acetylene Gas

The foremost British developer of vehicle lamps of all types was Joseph Lucas of Birmingham. By a brilliant stroke of inspiration he coined not only the phrase: 'We make light our labour', but also the widely used motto: 'King of the Road', which today has become a byword for quality of manufacture, featuring prominently in auction catalogues.

Although the French were the first to design such things, in about 1901 Lucas further developed the principal of dropping water onto calcium carbide to create acetylene gas, which, when lit, burnt with a brilliant white light. (The nearest thing to artificial daylight, it was claimed.) As vehicles became more reliable and speeds increased, a pair of Lucas 'King of the Road' head-lamps were employed to lighten the night sky. Costing £13 each in 1905, a good pair can easily fetch £1,000/$1,800 or more in the

salerooms today.

Another well-known British company was Powell and Hanmer. Like Lucas, this company have their roots firmly based in the 1880s and one is constantly being surprised by the variety and merit of their products. A single P & H headlamp sold at auction in 1981 for £190/$342; the same lamp today would achieve twice that. Deadly rivals until the depression of the late 1920s, Lucas paid £500,000 for P & H in 1929, fearing that a foreign competitor might purchase the ailing company and 'muscle in' on the lucrative market.

Below left Car meets provide ideal opportunities to purchase accessories and check details from other exhibits.

Below A good pair of Lucas self-contained Duplex headlamps. Introduced in 1907, they were manufactured until 1914. These lamps had a gas tap just below the burner to minimize burner-sooting under low pressure, and they carried two cylindrical containers of carbide. The left-hand one was a reserve supply, but if both were filled to capacity the lamps would burn for eight hours.

Bottom A magnificent pair of German Zeiss electric headlamps with correct supporting brackets still attached. The front glasses are superbly hand-cut and the shells are chromium-plated. Value: £800-£1,200/$1,440-$2,200. *Sotheby's*

Right A self-contained acetylene gas headlamp of the type manufactured between 1904 and 1914. Stirrup-mounted onto the front of a car, they would then be removed to allow for cleaning and charging with carbide. The hinged lid at the top covers the carbide holder and the water is poured into an unseen aperture at the rear. Often sold and used as a single lamp when new, today collectors expect to find them in matched pairs and will pay accordingly. Value: £100-£150/$180-$270 (single); £400-£600/$720-$1,080 (a pair).

Below the oil lamp on the left is one of a pair of 760 series side lamps, manufactured between 1907 and 1912. These lamps are eagerly sought because the front and side glasses are hand-cut. Should they be damaged, this will seriously affect their value of £150-£300/$270-$540 (a pair). Right: This Lucas 630 series lamp had a thirty-year production life from 1906. With a combination number plate and rear lamp, its value is about £80/$144.

As the motor car, and for that matter *voiturettes*, forecars and motorcycles, became more popular and easier to use, a new and vast industry supplying lamps grew in parallel. Two distinct types of acetylene lamp were evolved at this time. One was the type mentioned earlier, where the acetylene gas is created and burnt within the construction of the lamp itself. These are referred to as headlamps. The other type involved the use of one or more projectors; in this instance the gas was created in a separate generator, usually fitted to one of the running boards, where the controls would be within easy reach of the driver. A rubber tube would then transfer the gas to the lamp for igniting. The latter style

of illumination was more popular with French and American manufacturers. The Badger Brass company of America, for instance, offered solar models in about 1905; a fabulous pair of these projectors, albeit minus the appropriate gas generator, fetched £1,200/$2,200 at a recent sale.

Louis Blériot, who today is more famous for his pioneering activities in the air, also manufactured high quality headlamps and projectors before the Great War. Today his products are enthusiastically sought by the restorers of French-manufactured cars like De Dion-Bouton, Léon-Bollée and Voisin, and prices in the range of £300 to £800/$500-

Below Left: A Salsbury 'Flario' model self-contained acetylene gas headlamp, dating from around 1903. The Salsbury Company were the British pioneers of quality vehicle lighting and their products today are highly sought-after. A similar, single lamp recently fetched £800/$1,440 at auction. Right; Louis Blériot, the aviator, was also famous for manufacturing high quality lamps, during the early part of this century. This projector was designed as a spotlamp for a large commericial vehicle and, to enable an ever-stronger candle power to be produced, an oxy-acetylene gas was used. Note the burner track that allows for accurate focusing of the beam. Although well-made, cylindrical and perhaps staid lamps of this type are less pleasing to the eye and, consequently, do not achieve high sums at auction. Value: £50/$90 (single); £150/$270 (a pair).

$1,440 are not unusual for a good pair of Blériot headlamps.

In this modern age it is almost inconceivable that our forebears would trouble themselves with the preparation, use and necessary cleaning of these lamps. It must not be forgotten, however, that street lighting was minimal and the accident potential in daylight, let alone the hours of darkness, was much higher than it is today.

Despite the problems encountered with acetylene gas, headlamps were available throughout the early years of the motor car and up till the Second World War. It must be said however that the later (less well produced) examples were

specifically designed for use on commercial lorries and vans, and examples of these can be picked up for a few pounds.

Although a matching pair of lamps is aesthetically pleasing today, headlamps were not necessarily sold in pairs, particularly in the years prior to 1914. It is, nevertheless, true that at auction today a single example can often be purchased for about a quarter of the amount that a similar pair would fetch. While the idea of buying a single lamp from one venue, hoping to find a matching brother at some other sale or auto-jumble, appeals to the most thrifty soul, it can prove false economy. The fact is, the odds

against finding the correct partner, with similar detail of construction, are extremely high. This is because most manufacturers employed a policy of continuous change, in an effort to supply the perfect product.

Another now forgotten quality manufacturer to look out for is Salsbury; indeed, if contemporary photographs are any guide, practically all pre-1908 vehicles seem to have one or a pair of Salsbury 'Flario' lamps fitted. Perhaps an example of the esteem held for this company is reflected

in the £750/$1,350 price recently paid at auction for a single self-contained headlamp of this type.

Oil Lamps

While oil lamps were used as the sole illuminant on vehicles before the turn of the century, it was not long before their use was relegated to side lamps and, later, to rear lamps. The humble oil lamp, however, has over the years lent itself to some of the most interesting designs and styles. One type, which later became colloquially known as the 'opera lamp', reflects the days when such lamps were used as courtesy lights while the passengers alighted from vehicles in the dark, outside the theatre. One of the particular features of these lamps are the most attractive coloured and cut-glass side glasses. Reds, blues and sometimes greens are used and this, together with their neat appearance, makes for an excellent display. 'Opera lamps' were manufactured for a thirty year period from about 1910; today, at auction, they vary in value from about £100 to £300/

$180-$500 a pair.

Oil side-lamps come in various shapes and sizes. It is quite surprising how long, for instance, the Lucas 630, 720 and 740 series of lamps were advertised, a production run of thirty or more years not being unusual. Most lamps could be purchased with several alternative types of finish. Personally I prefer 'japanned' black with nickel-plated parts. However all nickel-plated or all chromium-plated (invented c.1927) looks most attractive, albeit originally costing an extra

Left A pair of French-manufactured benzoline lamps by Genies Frères. These lamps are finished in nickel over brass and have blue star-cut side glasses. Colloquially known as 'opera lamps', they were manufactured until the mid 1930s. A good pair will sell for about £150/$270.

shilling or two. All brass finish lamps were often available, but it must be said that it was not a popular finish in its day; it is a different story these days, however, when practically 75 per cent of all lamps offered are brass-finished. A point worth remembering when acquiring lamps is that they look better with their original finish, and showing their age, than if they have been highly polished.

Electric Lighting

Rotax and C.A.V. (Charles A. Vandervell) were both London-based companies, and achieved considerable success in their experimentation with electrically powered lamps before 1914. Their products are comparable with those from Lucas, but they were perhaps less stylized and aesthetically pleasing. Interestingly, both companies shared the same fate, being taken over by Lucas in the mid-1920s, although they continued to trade under their own names until 1939. The 1920s and 1930s are best described as the decades of the 'dip and switch'. The Government was alarmed at the increasing number of accidents on the roads and, in particular, accidents caused by the blinding effect of oncoming motorists' powerful headlamps. A plan was evolved whereby, upon the approach of a vehicle, the nearside electric headlamp would turn off and the offside lamp would dip to the kerb. As this system relied on a standard arrangement of switches and lamps the design and appearance of lighting equipment became very staid and uninteresting.

This twenty year period did have its highlights, however. In 1927 Lucas produced their now famous P100 range of lamps, which continued to be

Below A Triumph Dolomite with distinctive curved
radiator grille in chrome.

manufactured into the late 1950s. Interestingly, the reason why they were designated P100 was because they were designed to produce 100 candle power (a certain amount of advertising licence here!) and 'P' because they were intended for use on POSH cars such as the Rolls Royce, Mercedes and Bentley. A good pair of the earlier type will today command a figure of around £500/$900, whereas for later models fetch around £100/$180 a pair.

Further Developments

From the early days of motoring it had been a matter of personal preference as to exactly where lamps were fitted to vehicles. While oil and electric side-lamps were normally fitted to the sides of the car and either a single or pair of headlamps fitted to the front, this was by no means obligatory. By the late 1920s various regulations came into force and the outcome was the 'five lamp set': two evenly positioned headlamps, two parking or side lamps and one

rear combination number plate and stop tail lamp were introduced as standard equipment for all three and four wheeled vehicles until the outbreak of war in 1939. The pre-war years certainly proved to be the 'decade of motoring for the masses'.

Below Good quality flexible hose and trumpet bezel bulb horns are getting increasingly rare today, very often the rubber inner-tube is perished and the gauze and rim that covers the trumpet is missing. In excellent condition they will sell for about £400/$720, somewhat less if damaged. Lamp left: A Lucas P100 electric projector. The bulb is rear-facing and shines directly into the highly polished mirror at the rear. Value: £300/$540 (a pair). Lamp right: A single example of Lucas' Duplex self-contained acetylene gas lamp. Value: £200/$360 (single); £600/$1,080 (matched pair).

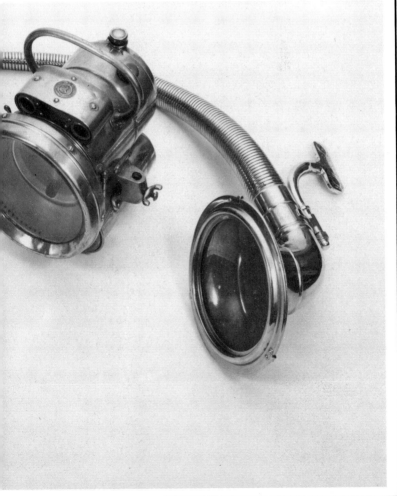

Chapter Five

Mascots

Since the very earliest days of the automobile man has sought to embellish and personalize his vehicle with some lucky charm or insignia that reflects his actual or perceived status in life. Certainly, as motoring became more affordable after about 1905 and vehicle design began to follow a set pattern, the urge to personalize one's vehicle, to differentiate it from similar examples, was, perhaps, inevitable. Various sculptors, particularly in France, began to offer an assortment of mascots. Some were extremely artistic and well-made, but other examples, particularly those offered through the many mail order catalogues that appeared during this time, were often outrageous and totally out of keeping with the vehicles they adorned.

Manufacturers' Approved Mascots

Things came to a head in 1910 when the directors of Rolls Royce were distressed to learn that talismans, from brass ornaments to small stuffed toys, were being attached to their cars. It was decided that a more dignified mascot should be designed, and

Below Top: The most famous of René Lalique's opalescent glass mascots: 'Victoire'. More often than not this is found damaged, particularly at the rear of the hair. This has often led to regrinding and polishing, which in turn shortens its length and affects its value. Value: £1,000-£5,000/$1,800-$9,000. Left to right: (a) An R.A.C. life member's badge of hollow construction and marked Elkington and Co. Ltd. Numbered A576, this 17 cm (6¾ in) high badge dates from 1910. Value: £400-£600/$720-$1.080. (b) Usually found in mascot form, this Singer Motors bantam is mounted on a manufactured base. Probably supplied as a trade gift, it was used as a paperweight. Value: £100-£150/$180-$270. (c) A china motorcyclist and motorcycle in action pose; well coloured and undamaged. Small attractive items like this are particularly popular. 11 cm (4¼ in) high. Value: £30-£50/$54-$90. (d) A lion designed by Steyr in France: an accessory mascot offered for use on a Peugeot motor car during the 1920s. 14 cm (5½ in) high. Value: £100-£200/$180-$360.

the famous English sculptor, Charles Sykes, was asked to invent a suitable emblem. 'The Spirit of Ecstasy', as it became known, has been fitted to all Rolls Royce cars until the present day. Although it was not the first manufacturers' mascot, it has certainly been the best known model in constant use. Ten main sizes have been issued during the last seventy years and various finishes have been supplied. Pre-1914 examples were often silver-plated, but nickel-plating was in use until the late 1920s and chrome-plating from then until the mid-1950s, after which stainless steel was employed.

It is believed that the Vulcan Motor Company offered the first manufacturers' mascot, that of Vulcan the blacksmith, in about 1903. But it was not until after the First World War that other

Below Three examples of the artistry of René Lalique, from left to right: *'Chrysis'*, or nude, in frosted glass, 13 cm (5 in) high; value £300-£600/$540-$1,080. *'Tête de Coq'*, or cock's head, 19 cm (7½ in) high (the cock's comb is often found damaged and re-cut); value: £400-£800/$720-$1,440. *'Tête d'Aigle'*, or eagle's head, a clear glass mascot never intended as such but apparently used by Third Reich officers on their staff cars; value: £400-£800/$720-$1,440. These mascots, along with several others, were also supplied unmounted as paperweights.

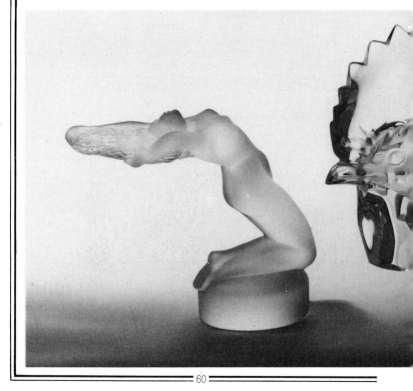

manufacturers began to offer an approved emblem for their products. Following in the footsteps of Vulcan, other companies turned to heraldry and mythology as sources of inspiration: The Farman Company using Icarus, Minerva using the head of the goddess, Vauxhall the Wyvern and Unic various interpretations of a centaur holding a bow.

Animals were also a popular subject with manufacturers, the most famous being the various interpretations of a flying stork used by Hispano-Suiza. The source of inspiration for this mascot was the Cigogne-Volante emblem that Guynemer's Escadrille N.3 squadron of First World War flying aces used on their aircraft, powered, co-incidentally, by Hispano-Suiza engines. Other examples were

Alvis and their seated hare, Ford with a bantam in flight (a bust of Henry was also available) and Jaguar's leaping cat, which they used from 1945. This is thought to have been inspired by Cecil Kimber's short-lived 18/100 or Tigress model.

Accessory Mascots

The other main category of mascot is the proprietary or accessory mascot which has been manufactured for almost as long as the motor car itself. These were made available in many thousands of different styles and shapes over the years and, today, offer the collector a wide choice, particularly if he chooses to limit himself to a thematic collection, be it the work of a particular sculptor, animal/novelty types or naked females. The quality of manufacture and artistic merit can

vary enormously, as can the quality of the finish.

For ease of identification, these mascots can be sub-divided into various categories:

Glass Mascots

The most spectacular and innovative of mascots were those designed and marketed by René Jules Lalique. Born in 1860, he was a jeweller by trade who later discovered the artistic qualities of glass. In 1925 Lalique was commissioned to design a glass mascot for the Citroën Company The car, and subsequently the mascot, were called Cinq Chevaux (five horses) and was an immediate success with elegant French society. Over thirty further mascots were designed over the following five years, ranging in appearance from the downright

whimsical to the truly symbolic. Adverse reaction, however, was levied against Lalique's mascots, particularly by the magazine *Art et Industrie* in 1928, when they reported: 'And, on the radiator cap, an objet d'art in glass; destined to be smashed one day by a spanner! . . . we must get rid of all the junk!' Junk indeed! Despite the bad press these mascots were in popular demand

Below The unmistakable grille of a Rolls Royce 'Phantom', crowned by the world famous mascot.

and, in England, Lalique's London
agents, the Brèves Galleries, were
highly successful in marketing the
mascots to smart English society.
The most common method of
mounting the mascot was to attach
it directly to the radiator cap.
Another method was to set the
ornament further back on the
bonnet and, quite often, the
Brèves Gallery illuminated mount
would be used to great effect. This
took the form of a nickel-plated
base incorporating a bulb and
coloured filters (usually green,
blue and amber). When switched
on through the dynamo system the
warm glow of light would
illuminate the glass and increase
in light intensity as the speed of
the vehicle increased.

The most successful of Lalique's
mascot designs must be his
'Victoire', which was also known
as 'Spirit of the Wind', or 'Seminole'
in the U.S.A. Often termed the
'Rolls Royce mascot', because of
its frequent use on expensive cars,
it is, nevertheless, a superb design
achievement and wholly
appropriate for its function.
An undamaged example will
fetch about £5,000/$9,000 in a
saleroom today.

It is said that imitation is the
sincerest form of flattery, and so it
was that various firms attempted
to emulate the superb range of
Lalique products. Red Ashay was
a British company that came
close to equalling the Lalique
quality. Various similar models
were produced: a female head
with flowing hair to rival 'Victoire',
a nude kneeling figure similar to
Lalique's 'Chrysis' and, perhaps
their most famous, the 'Butterfly
Girl', a well-detailed female figure
with outstretched wings. These
mascots could also be supplied
with illuminated bases.

Right Poetry in motion: this nicely patinated bronze
model of a scantily-clad female dancing in the wind
was designed by Sykes, who was also the designer
of the Rolls Royce mascot. Named the 'Speed of the
Wind', it was exhibited at the Paris Salon de Beaux
Arts before the Great War. 19 cm (7½ in) high,
including base. Value: £200-£300/$360-$540.

Left A selection of highly collectable automobilia including car badges, postcards, mascots, printed literature and playing cards.

In recent years a Czechoslovakian glass company has produced frosted glass mascots under the 'Bohemia' trade name. Costing about £100/$180 new, some unscrupulous traders are unfortunately having 'R. Lalique' etched into the base and passing them off as originals. So, if you are ever offered such items and the quality is suspect, it is worth remembering that most genuine Lalique mascots have 'R. Lalique' *moulded* into the glass, usually around the base.

Metal mascots

By far the largest selection of mascots available to the enthusiast will fall into this category. These mascots were created by an accessory company not for any particular vehicle (although there are exceptions which we will discuss later). They were simply supplied to embellish a car and probably reflected more the personality of the owner than the honour of the vehicle's manufacturers. Often bought from outlets such as Halfords' or Currys', the larger department stores also offer a wide choice. A budding ornithologist can select a bird from a range varying from an eagle in full flight to a stylized and aggressive-looking cockatoo. Copies of the Hispano-Suiza stork also abound, each with a long neck and pointed head: a dangerous addition to the radiator cap, should the car be involved in a collision with a pedestrian. It would most certainly infringe regulations if mounted on a modern car. This safety aspect was identified as early as the 1930s; in response to public pressure the Desmo Company produced a stork in full flight, but with a rubber neck! A novelty item well worth searching for.

Another novelty bird was that manufactured by Flying Mascots Ltd. of 199 Piccadilly, London. This chrome-on-brass mascot had the ability to flap its wings while the vehicle was in forward motion, the air flow activating the wings as if the bird was actually in flight.

For those collectors interested in novelty mascots, the illustrator John Hassel created several character mascots which had egg-shaped heads of dark brown porcelain, with painted features which could be altered into various poses. The most popular is his policeman 'Robert' (c. 1920) standing 11.5cm (4½in) high and selling for about £200/$360 at auction. A mascot that would not have endeared itself to the local constabulary in the past, it is now most popular with policeman collectors of my acquaintance. Other policeman mascots have

been issued over the years; these are usually shown with an arm outstretched in regulation manner.

Dogs have always been popular, pehaps more so with kennel clubs and the like. Scottie dogs and poodles abound in large numbers, again usually distributed by the Desmo Company. But the most popular dog mascot in the 1920s and 1930s was the patriotic British bulldog. Obtainable in various poses – standing, sitting and running – the best known mascot of this type must be 'Bonzo', the cartoon character bull terrier puppy.

Left A large bronze statue of Icarus was originally crafted by George Colin in celebration of the first winged flight of Santos-Dumont. In later years the Farman company adopted the model as the company emblem. The mascot shown was supplied by Finnigans of London.

Below Fun and whimsical mascots have become more popular in recent years, with bronze characters like this 'Minnie Mouse' mascot achieving the best results. Value: £100-£150/$180-$270.

Below Left to right: (a) An R.A.C. associate club badge with a central enamelled device for the Automobile Club of Victoria (Australia); dating from c.1910, it is very rare. Value: £100-£150/$180-$270. (b) A Rolls Royce mascot designed for the 20 hp model. Standing 12.5 cm (5 in) high, there is an inscribed registration date of 1911 around the base, and U.S. patent office marks beneath the wings. (c) A noticeably larger Rolls Royce mascot mounted on an incorrect radiator cap but suitable for the 40/50 hp ('Silver Ghost') car. 17 cm (6¾ in) high.

Value: £150-£300/$270-$540. Both the Rolls Royce mascots have their original nickel plate and are in fine condition. Replated examples and figures that have been bent or damaged will be worth considerably less. (d) A winged nymph and wheel accessory mascot dating from the middle 1930s. Value: £20-£30/$36-$54. (e) A nickel on brass ski lady; the designated Riley emblem, but also very popular with the 'smart set' who ventured to the Alps every year, with or without their cloche hats!

Above left The popular 'Archer', by Lalique, which was often adopted by the owners of Pierce-Arrow cars. Value: £500-£600/$900-$1,080.

Below A lovingly-restored Austin in full working order. Note the split windscreen for efficient ventilation.

Most metal mascots could be purchased with a choice of finishes. Although before *c.* 1928 nickel plate and polished brass were available, the hardness and durability of chrome plating was popular throughout the '30s. Very often mascots receive the attentions of the restorer who, upon finding a good but poorly finished mascot, will have it replated. There are two reasons why this should be avoided. Firstly, like so many artefacts of automobilia it is better that a mascot be left as found, with all the warts and scars that only age can inflict. In other words, the integrity of the piece should be left intact. In this day and age when metal mascots are being reproduced, it could be argued that the re-plater is trying to hide something! Secondly, replating in either chrome or nickel (and sometimes silver) means that the mascot has to be stripped and polished. This can mean, particularly in the hands of a less than sympathetic polisher, that corners and features are polished away, so much so, in some cases, that the once excellent detailed crafting has been ruined. In short, it is better to buy a mascot showing its years than something you can see your reflection in.

Dual purpose accessory mascots

Some mascots, by accident or design, could be fitted to specific models of car. Indeed, this is positively encouraged by some car manufacturers. The Desmo's leaping jaguar (as distinct from the later official Jaguar mascot, fitted in the 40s) was designed to fit the SS80 and SS100 models with the blessing of the Jaguar company, in the 1937 to 1939 period. Examples would sell at auction for between £120 and £180/$220-$324. French designer, Steyr, created a standing lion with its paw on a globe; this was specifically manufactured for the Peugeot motor car, although it was never officially adopted by the factory. There are many other examples, perhaps some still lying dormant, waiting to be identified.

Below Left to right: (a) A good nickel on brass policeman mascot of the type popular just after the Great War. Value: £80-£100/$144-$180. (b) Naked females abound in all shapes, styles and poses. This example is called 'Hello Nymph', by the A. E.

Liversedge company. Value: £60-£80/$108-$144. (c) A very rare, fully-equipped knight holding a banner with the word 'Phronimos' inscribed. This mascot was used on Sentinel commercial vehicles during the 1920s. 17 cm (6¾ in) high. Value £150-£200/$270-$360.

Top left Created in the cubist style, this set of three American 'Mack' bulldog mascots have been artistically mounted on a polished wooden display base. Value: £50-£60/$90-$180.

Top right Created by Bruce Bainsfather, the famous Great War cartoonist, 'Ole Bill' appeared during the 1920s as a car mascot. Available in two sizes, the larger example, 10 cm (4 in) high, is valued at £100-£150/$180-$270.

Middle Cleverly using their slogan 'Feathers in our cap', the Guy Motors mascot was originally cold-painted. Today, however, reproductions abound and this has resulted in the original mascot's reduced value.

Below An amusing (for some) nickel-on-brass skull and cross-bones mascot, with a fitting at the base for illumination (a rare sight at the dead of night). Value: £50-£100/$90-$180.

Chapter Six

Badges and Awards

Man has always sought to identify himself with some chosen group or body of people, if only to demonstrate his affinity to the regulations and creed that he wishes to uphold. It may indeed be élitism, snobbery, call it what you will, but to apply an insignia to your favourite oil-powered steed proves, perhaps, that man is but a pack animal.

Club Badges

The Automobile Club of Great Britain and Ireland was founded by F. R. Simms, one of this country's motoring visionaries, in 1897. He also founded the Society of Motor Manufacturers and Traders and it could even be argued that he founded the British Motor Industry itself! The club went from strength to strength

Below Left to Right: (a) A nickel on brass and multi-coloured enamel National Motorists Association full members badge, numbered 2038, and marketed through Collins of London. Notice the Latin inscription Omnium Saluti. Value: £80/$144. (b) A flying B radiator mascot designed for use on the two most popular Derby Bentleys, the 3½ litre and 4½ litre models. This mascot has been replated, and the heavily polished and damaged feather detail can be seen if one compares it with the next example. Value: £30-£50/$54-$90 (polished); £50-£100/$90-$180 (unpolished). (c) A post-World War II Bentley mascot suitable for fitting to the R-type and later Mark VI Bentleys; excellent original condition. Value: £50-£80/$90-$144. (d) Called the Cyclecar Club before the Great War, this club was reformed and renamed the Junior Car Club in 1919. In 1946 it joined with the B.A.R.C. to form the British Automobile Racing Club, but in the intervening years it serviced the racing interests of cycle and light car owners. The J.C.C. club badge is quite rare today and in good condition will achieve about £80/$144 at auction.

and, in 1907, was offered royal patronage when Edward VII agreed to become its patron; it was thereafter called the Royal Automobile Club (RAC). The new full members' badge consisted of a crowned motor wheel, centred with a bust of Edward VII and supported by a winged torso of Mercury. The early badge measures 17cm (6½in) high and will command a figure of around £500/$900 at auction. It must not, however, be confused with the smaller but similar badge with the Queen's crown attached, which is still issued to full members today. At about this time various regional motor clubs were allowed to become associates of the club. The standard circular members' badge had an enamelled centre

proudly bearing the arms of the associated club. Today these badges are highly collected, with affiliations such as The North Eastern Automobile Association or The South Wales Association fetching about £130/$234 at an auction sale.

The other major British motoring club is, of course, the Automobile Association (AA). The familiar entwined double 'A' first appeared in about 1906. The peculiarity of this early example is that the signature of the first secretary, Stenson Cooke, is embossed on the bracket. A 'Stenson Cooke' as they are affectionately known, will cost between £80-£120/$144-$220 at

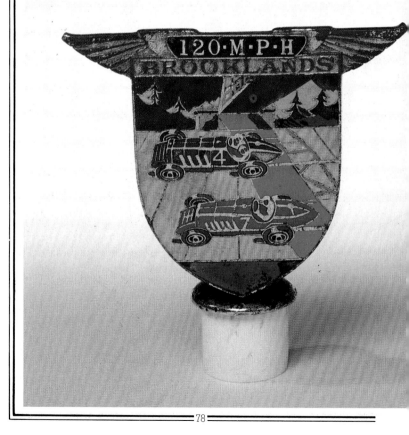

auction depending on condition. One word of warning, however, is that these plain brass insignia are now being reproduced and passed off as originals. If the badge does not have the patina that only age can produce, steer well clear of it!

Perhaps the most interesting feature of collecting badges is that they can be very colourful and will make a most impressive display. The deep red enamel of the 'Order of the Road' members badge is most attractive and worth about £50/$90, if it has the correct hinged tab stating 'member not driving' and a date plaque.

The most sought-after club badges are those associated with

Below Right: The standard B.A.R.C. members badge, depicting two racing cars on the Brooklands banking beneath the members bridge. These badges, in good condition, will sell for about £400-£600/$720-$1,080 today, although originally they cost £1! Left: Basically the standard B.A.R.C. members badge, but including a 120 mph tablet instead of B.A.R.C. This particular badge was awarded to Norman Black, who, on 22nd September 1934, achieved a speed of over 120 mph on the Brooklands circuit, driving an Alfa Romeo. The rear of the badge is duly inscribed. Although it will be seen from the illustration that the upper enamelled area is badly damaged, this item achieved a price of £1,400/$2,520 at auction in 1987.

the Brooklands track. The Brooklands Automobile Racing Club was founded in 1907 (following its closure in 1939, it was reformed in 1950 as the British Automobile Racing Club) and the badges issued during the 20s are superb works of art. The scene depicted in various shades of enamel is of two racing cars on the banking passing beneath the members bridge. The words 'B.A.R.C.' and 'Brooklands' are positioned at the top of the shield shape. In good condition the badge today will achieve £400-£600/$720-$1,100. Variations of this badge were given to drivers who lapped the track at over 120 mph. These badges were awarded between 1921 and 1938 and only seventeen 130 mph badges were

awarded between 1930 and 1939. In each case either an 120 mph or 130 mph tablet replaced B.A.R.C., and the recipient's name and date of performance are inscribed on the rear. A 130 mph badge, awarded to R. R. K. Marker in 1936, recently sold for £3,800/$6,840 at auction.

At the other end of the price scale there is a vast selection of modestly priced club badges available to the collector. The great number of small clubs that have existed through the years each had their own badge. Some of these are exquisitely crafted, while others are barely recognizable as a badge at all. However, most would make interesting and bright additions to any collection.

Left A collection of twelve various motoring medallions: four from the Junior Car Club and the remainder from various other provincial clubs. Value: £120-£150/$220-$270.

Below The Muratti Trophy. Fashioned in silver and assayed at Sheffield in 1904, this beautifully-crafted trophy was presented by the cigarette manufacturers B. Muratti, Sons & Co. to the Motorcycle Union of Ireland. The modeller seems to have based the trophy on a Bradbury motorcycle; the component fittings, such as carburettor, oil feed, pedals and exhaust are all accurately reproduced. The trophy sold at auction in 1987 for £12,000/ $21,600.

Below right A colourful and varied selection of car rally badges of the past.

Other Badges

Not all badges which have been attached to vehicles were mounted for the enjoyment of pedestrians. A particular favourite of mine are the small retailers', badges attached to the dashboard of the car. One finely enamelled example I have seen announces, 'Purchased from Holloways, coachbuilders and purveyors of fine vehicles to motorists'. Highly prized by collectors are similar badges from such firms as Strachans, Mann-Egerton, and the like. Once eagerly hunted in scrap yards because nobody but a mad collector would tip the man at the gate for an interesting handful, today prices vary between £25 and £150/$45-$270, and if you are lucky enough to find a silver example, you may need to take out a bank loan!

Rally Plaques

Made popular in the height of the international rally scene

during the 1930s, these were given to competitors for mounting upon the vehicle's dashboard. Found in all shapes and sizes, some plain while others were very colourful due to the applied enamel, all are extremely well crafted and attractive. They usually depict some motoring scene, with the name of the event and date moulded into the alloy casting. Eagerly collected by enthusiasts today, modern equivalents are now presented at veteran and vintage rallies. Varying in price from £20 to £200/$36-$360, every auction will produce a few examples; so why not see how many you can find.

Cups and Trophies

Competition motoring has always produced personalities, spectacular events and, of course, winners. In parallel with these races and rallies were the supply of prizes that match the importance and appeal of the

Right An Automobile Association car badge, presented to a member. This familiar emblem is popular with collectors.

Below right A 'Stenson Cooke' AA badge, dating from about 1909.

event. For a local speed event a medallion would be enscribed with the date and winner's name, while, on the other hand, a cup of magnificent proportions would be presented to the winner of, for example, a British Racing Drivers 500 mile race at Brooklands. The value of such items does depend very much on the provenance and uniqueness of each piece. A small silver cup was sold recently at Phillips; it was the third prize at the June Sprint Race held on 17 June 1911 and was won by a Mr P. Lambert, driving an Austin. This 8oz cup has a basic market value of £40/$72, until one realises, however, that the Mr Lambert mentioned was a famous early lap and distance record driver and was not only the first driver to exceed 100 mph, but was killed in 1913 in an attempt to break the one hour record, also at Brooklands. Because of this provenance the trophy achieved a much higher figure at auction.

In contrast a 22ct gold medal, given at about the same time for a little known event to an unknown driver, will achieve little more than scrap value. Such is life, although it may be a good tip for the enthusiast looking for an untapped field!

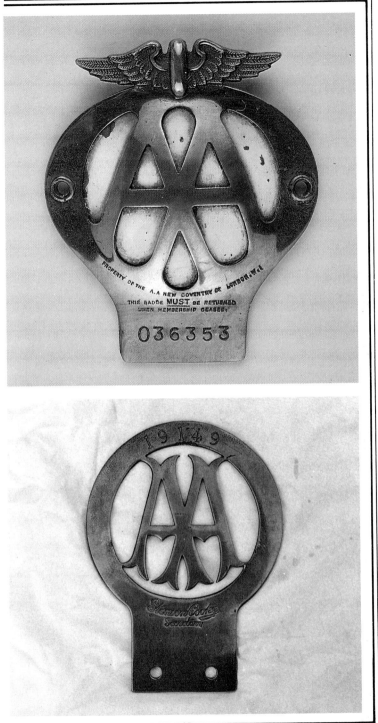

Chapter Seven

Assorted Treasures

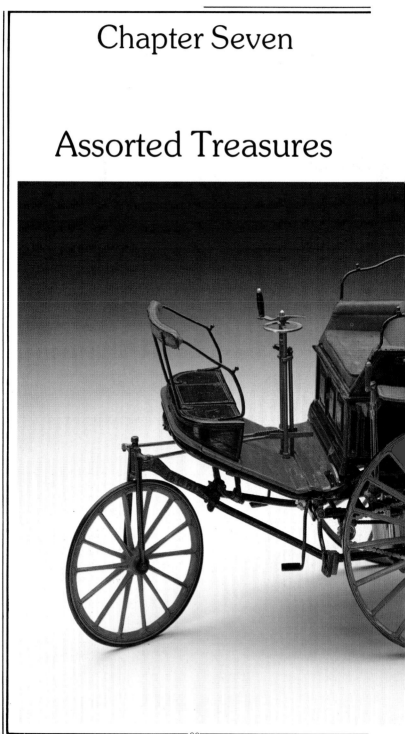

Below A well-constructed scratch-built model of a c.1888 Benz tricycle. The model includes all the major components and fittings, and was built by the late F. J. Camm, journalist and editor. Value: £3,000-£5,000/$5,400-$9,000.

This chapter will attempt to deal with some of those items that are not covered by previous headings but are, nevertheless, interesting and worth adding to your collection.

Motor Clothing

In the days before the Great War cars were generally of the open-tourer variety, and some protection was required to keep out the wet and cold and, not least, the dust from the unmetalled roads. Ankle length leather coats for men were considered sartorially correct and, for ladies, fur coats and stoles and small hats with gauze veils were the order of the day. Good quality clothing from this period does turn up from time to time and will usually be valued from between £50 and £150/$90-$270. Although in the early days yachting caps were very popular for men, the leather flying helmet is today associated with competition motoring and these, together with goggles, can be bought for about £20/$36 at auction. The one item that is good fun to find is the kid-lined, leather *full* face mask, 'for ladies who wished to preserve their complexions'. An item of ridicule even at the time, examples are rare today.

Above One could be forgiven for not realising that this is an advertisement for Mumm Champagne. A superb lithographic poster by Rossi, it shows a group of Edwardian motorists taking an enforced stop with their rear-entrance tonneau car. A picnic awaits them! Value: £30-£50/$54-$90.

Picnic Sets

One item that has recently attracted more interest, and therefore higher prices, than any other motoring item, is the picnic set. Available in all shapes and sizes, from a unit catering for six with spirit fire, kettle, teapot and plates, to a two-man device housing a flask for hot water and two mugs, plates, sandwich box and milk flask, they range in value from £50-£1500/$90-$2,700. The most important factor is the general completeness and condition of the artefacts; clearly a hamper with half its fitted contents missing and little hope of finding correct replacements will be worth practically nothing. A full and undamaged set bearing the Fortnum and Mason insignia, however, is a joy to behold.

Dashboard Instruments

Various types of dialled instruments have been available since the birth of the car.

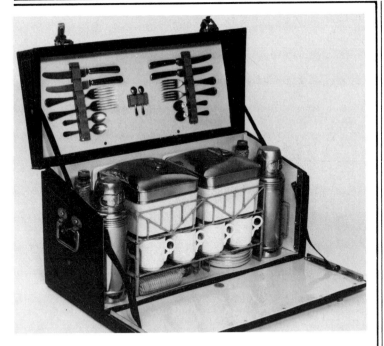

Commercially manufactured speedometers were available from about 1903 when more and more motorists were being fined for 'furious driving'. Jones' of America, like Smiths' in England, were the first manufacturers of quality instruments, which are keenly sought by collectors today. Modern cars have the speedometer and odometer combined as one unit, but before the Great War they could be purchased separately and a trip recorder was an optional extra. For the racing or sports car, revolution counters or tachometers were often fitted and usually took their drive from the rear of the camshaft.

Before the days when such aids to driving were flush-fitted into the front fascia of the car, early examples were either mounted onto the steering wheel column or were screwed directly into the wooden dash.

The clock has always been

Above A superbly fitted picnic hamper sold through Drew and Sons of Piccadilly, London and including practically everything a touring party of four would need for a luncheon stop on the moors! Value: £500-£800/$900-$1,440.

popular with motorists. Veteran examples usually consist of large watches fitted into a brass angled case. Similar clocks were also available for fitting onto motorcycles. Prices will vary from £50 to £200/$90-$360, depending on condition and completeness of the item.

Garage Equipment and Tools

Apart from the more obvious pieces of hardware like bottle jacks, foot pumps, petrol pumps and the like, there are many other less obvious items that were once commonplace. Often fitted into leather or polished wood boxes, some were very well made. The Vulcaniser, for example, has long since vanished from the scene, but in its day it was frequently employed to mend punctures, either at the roadside or garage. An electrical testing set was often used when electric lighting started to gain favour in the 1920s. Inspection lamps can also be found in many ingenious shapes and patterns.

Perhaps the nicest aspect of this field of collecting is that, although not as aesthetically pleasing as the other forms of automobilia, good quality, obsolete tools can still be purchased quite cheaply and are in plentiful supply at auto-jumbles and the like. A brass stirrup pump,

for example, can still be found for about £5/$9, and a Pyrene brass-plated fire extinguisher of the type frequently carried in vehicles in the 1930s, for about £8/$14.

Old spanners and special tools are still quite practical items, but are more eagerly sought,

Below Left to right: (a) A Silkolene motor oils pyramid-shaped tin, in excellent condition. Value: £40-£60/$72-$108. (b) A Shell petrol pump globe, dated 1950. Value: £50-£80/$90-$144. (c) This N.O.L. oil can would have been standard equipment on all Morris and Wolsey cars in the late 1930s. Value: £10-£15/$18-$27. (d) A brass exhaust whistle in unrestored condition. Value: £40-£60/$72-$108.

Below right Dating from c. 1902, an early form of folding travelling clock with a hand-painted motoring scene on porcelain. Value: £100-£200/$180-$360.

particularly if they have the make of car, for which they were originally designed, moulded into their construction. For instance, spanners marked Darracq will often change hands for £20/$36, or more, and spanners marked Swift or Chater Lea are rare. Rolls Royce or Austin, on the other hand, are in more plentiful supply, and a good selection can be put together for a few pounds.

Unquestionably, this is an area of automobilia collecting that can reap dividends if your are persistent and leave no tool box unturned. There is many a gem yet to be found, but the greatest attraction will be that an interesting and varied collection need not cost the owner a fortune.

Horns

Horns fall into two main categories: bulb horns and mechanical horns. The former have been offered in accessory catalogues since the earliest days. This basic variety consisted of a rubber bulb fitted to the end of a stem, which could either be straight, multi-turned or a flexible length of metal hose with a rubber liner. The last two types produced a much higher and more audible note. The device ended in a trumpet of some type, although the various types of serpent head are today most popular. Prices will vary considerably, with the more basic horns selling for between £10 and £50/$18-$90 and the more spectacular examples about £300/$540. It must be remembered, however, that Indian manufacturers using old style insignia and styles are manufacturing reproductions. These are often proffered as originals but are easily identified by the pale coloured, high zinc content brass used; if in doubt refuse it.

The electro-mechanical type of horns have been available since about 1905 from manufacturers such as C.A.V. and Lucas. Using a 6 and 12 volt current, an electrical motor vibrates a metal membrane,

Right Clockwise order: (a) A flexible hose bulb horn, labelled 'Boa Constrictor'; in poor condition. Value: £50-£100/$90-$180. (b) An Elliot 'double clock', combining speedo and trip milometer, as fitted to the dashboard of veteran cars. This is a most rare device, particularly if the flexible drive and gearing are intact. Value: £1,000-£1,500/$1,800-$2,700. (c) A multi-turn built horn with correct trumpet gauze fitted. (d) An electrical type pump, incorporating a pressure gauge and 'Mr. Bibendum' mascot seated on the compressor. (e) A travelling representative's demonstration model of a lifting jack, complete with miniature cranking handle and release valve. A fun item and, like other trade items, highly collectable. Value: £50-£100/$90-$180.

Right A Lucas double turn bulb horn of the type that was manufactured from the early 1920s until after the Second World War. Value: £30/$54.

the pitch of which is governed by the speed and pressure of the motor. Like so many household trade names that today represent a whole field of devices, these horns are usually referred to by the most popular trade name of Klaxon. Trumpet horns of this type were made well into the 1960s, but early examples will range in value from about £20/$36 to a multi-trumpet luxury type which may sell for £200/$360 or more. The hand-powered horns work on the same principle as the latter type, but a spinning flywheel takes the place of the motor.

Oil and Petrol Cans

The most colourful of forecourt equipment, the once ubiquitous, rectangular-shaped petrol cans have been collected for many years. Names like Pratts, Esso and Shell are most often found embossed into the side, along with the matching brass-threaded cap covering the pouring hole. Most often found today repainted and possibly rusty, the real rarities are the unspoilt examples with original finish. Other rarities that can be found by the persistent enthusiast, particularly at boot fairs and jumble sales, where an unusual can will not necessarily be recognised, are Aeroshell, Atlantic, Power Spirit, etc. The extra bonus in terms of identifying petrol cans is that they were often

code dated on their base. Next time you see one of the rectangular-shaped cans, turn it over and three of four numbers will be seen. If, for example, 636 is shown then the manufactured date will be June 1936; if, on the other hand, 1230 is seen, December 1930 will be the date. This system also applies to petrol pump glass globes, but the numerals are painted around the neck.

There is a very wide choice of illustrated cans of all types and prices will vary from about £5 to £50/$9-$90, depending on condition and rarity. One word of advice: in my opinion, it is better to pay £50/$90 for a can in pristine condition than to purchase ten heavily over-painted cans, which have seen better days, for the

same price.

In conclusion, let me outline a number of other collecting areas that are worthy of consideration, but by their nature are not directly related to automobilia. Cigarette cards are an interesting example, and should anyone wish to collect cards connected with motoring he has a wide and very colourful choice. 78rpm records and sheet music is another odd-ball area. Perhaps difficult to find, there have, nevertheless, been a large number of songs issued over the years, with titles like 'In my little Austin Seven', 'My Merrie Oldsmobile' and 'Maurice and his Morris'. Finally, pedal cars and toys are perhaps the one form of automobilia which everybody has owned at sometime; a collection

of such items can be a most colourful and rewarding specialization. The author can recommend the companion volume to this concerning tin toys (by Nigel Mynheer), as excellent further reading for collectors in this field.

Below Lithographed tin plate toys have always been popular. The variety and quality of such items can only be marvelled at, and any good toy sale will have a good selection available. As this photo shows, the best buys are those toys in need of some repair. But, like so many collectables, you only get what you pay for; it is not unusual to pay £5,000/$9,000 or more, for example, for a veteran Guntherman or Märklin limousine in superb condition, with original transfer work, hand-finishing and clockwork motor.

Bibliography

Barty-King, H., *The A.A. — A History of the First 75 Years*, A.A., 1980
Card, P.W., *Early Vehicle Lighting*, Shire Publications, 1987
Card, P.W., *Lucas the First King of the Road*, Privately printed, 1985
Gardiner, Gordon and Morris, Alistair, *The Price Guide and Identification of Automobilia*, Antique Collectors Club, 1982
Mynheer, N., *The Phillips Guide to Tin Toys*, Boxtree Ltd.
Nicholson, T.R., *Car Badges of the World*, Cassell, London
Pressland, David, *The Art of the Tin Toy*, New Cavendish Books, London
Roberts, Peter, *Any Colour so Long as it's Black*, David and Charles, 1976
Sirignano and Sulzberger, *Car Mascots*, Macdonald and Janes, London
Tubbs, D.B., *Art and the Automobile*, Lutterworth Press, London, 1987
Worthington-Williams, M., *Automobilia — A Guided Tour for Collectors*, R.A.C. and Batford, London 1979.

Places to visit

Automobilia, Billy Lane, Old Town, Hebden Bridge, West Yorks. Tel: 042284 4775
British Motor Industry Heritage Trust, Heritage Collection, Syon Park, Brentford, Middlesex TW8 8JF. Tel: 01-560 1378
Cotswold Motor Museum, The Old Mill, Bourton-on-the-Water, Glos. Tel: 0451 21255
Manx Motor Museum, Crosby, Isle of Man. Tel: 0624 851236
Melrose Motor Museum, Annay Road, Melrose, Roxburgh TD6 9LW. Tel: 089682 2624
National Motor Museum, Beaulieu, Brockenhurst, Hants SO4 7ZN. Tel: 0590 612345
Peter Black Collection, Keighley, West Yorks. Tel: 0535 61177 (appointment only)
Science Museum, Exhibition Road, S. Kensington, London SW7 2DD. Tel: 01-589 3456

Acknowledgements

The author's thanks go to Chris Halton, Diana Kay and Jacqueline Barber in the photographic archives at Phillips. The photographs in this book were supplied by Phillips, the author and David Card.

Picture Acknowledgements

Dunestyle Publishing Ltd., Title page, 7, 19, 55, 62, 63.

To my wife, Susan.